Psycho Color 2

24 Patterns to Spark
Your Imagination

by

Vincent Van Gouache

Psycho Color 2

The human mind has developed a unique ability to recognize patterns. It is for this reason we see animals in the clouds and beauty in the rippled sand along a deserted beach.

Relax. Breathe deeply. Let your mind clear.

Then, when you're ready, add colors that suit your mood to the patterns in this book. Let your mind wander, daydream. A creative spirit exists in each of us. Embrace it. — Vincent

Second Edition

ISBN-13: 978-1523739646
ISBN-10: 1523739649

INDEX

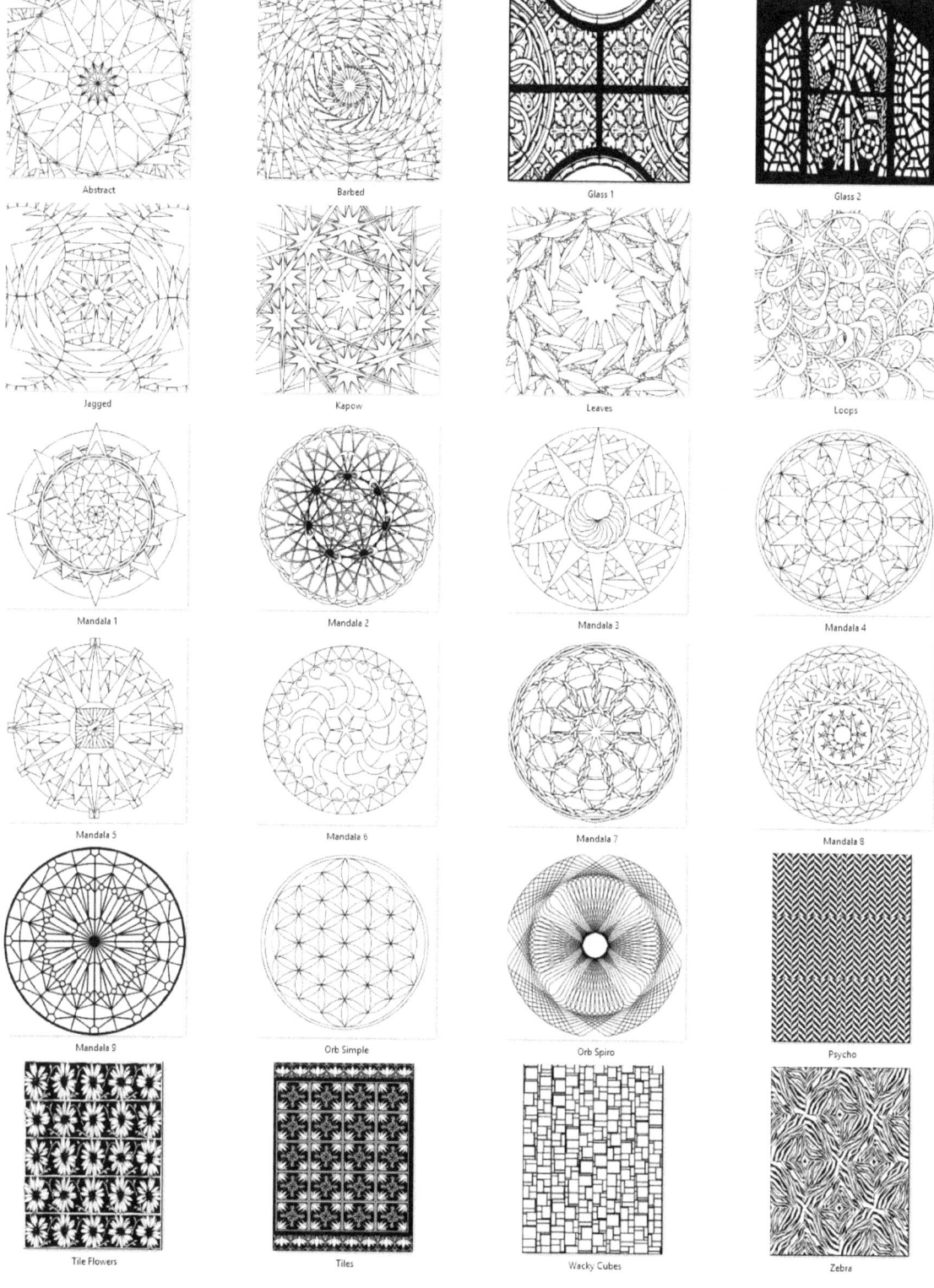

Abstract

Barbed

Glass 1

Glass 2

Jagged

Kapow

Leaves

Loops

Mandala 1

Mandala 2

Mandala 3

Mandala 4

Mandala 5

Mandala 6

Mandala 7

Mandala 8

Mandala 9

Orb Simple

Orb Spiro

Psycho

Tile Flowers

Tiles

Wacky Cubes

Zebra

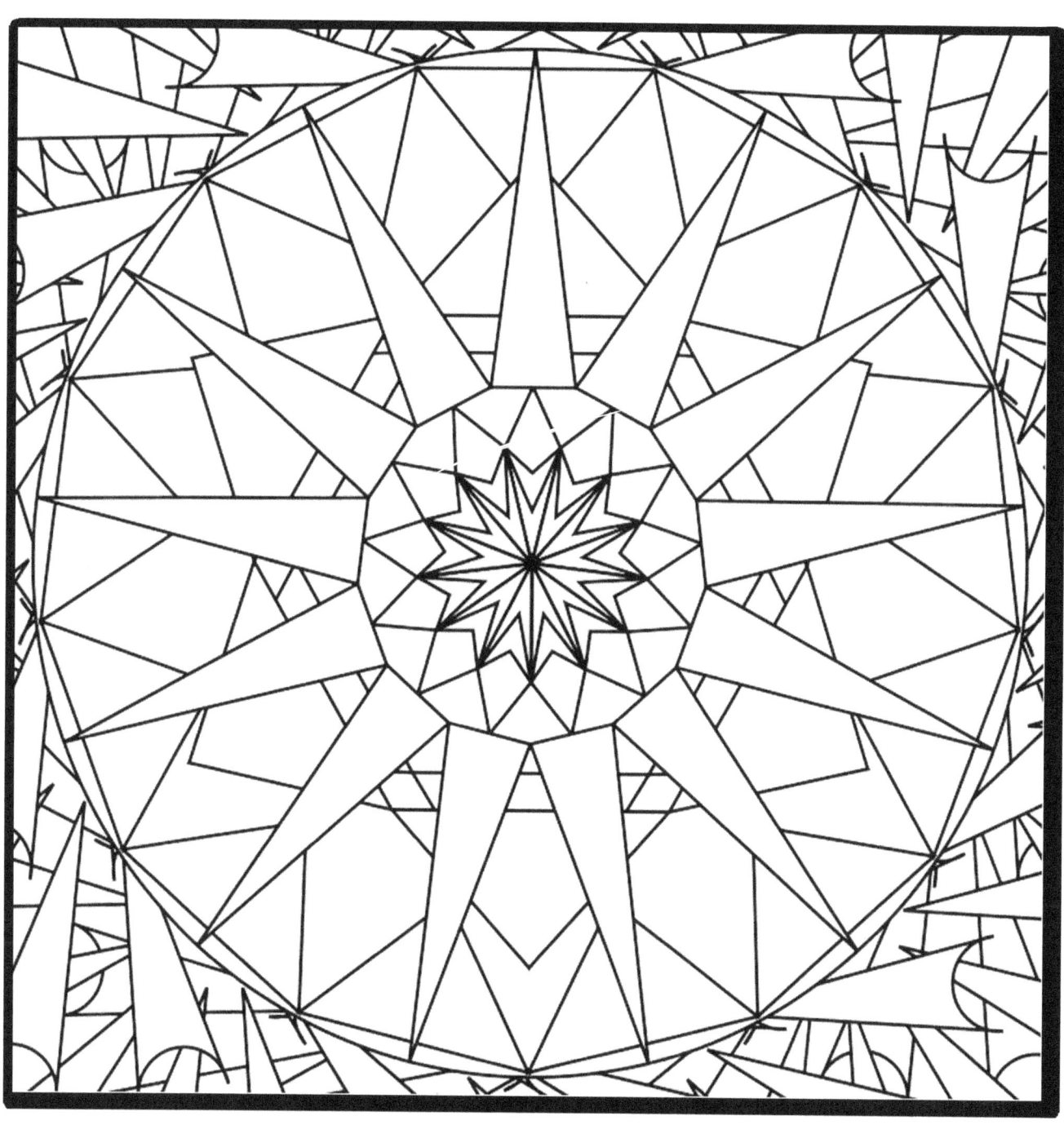

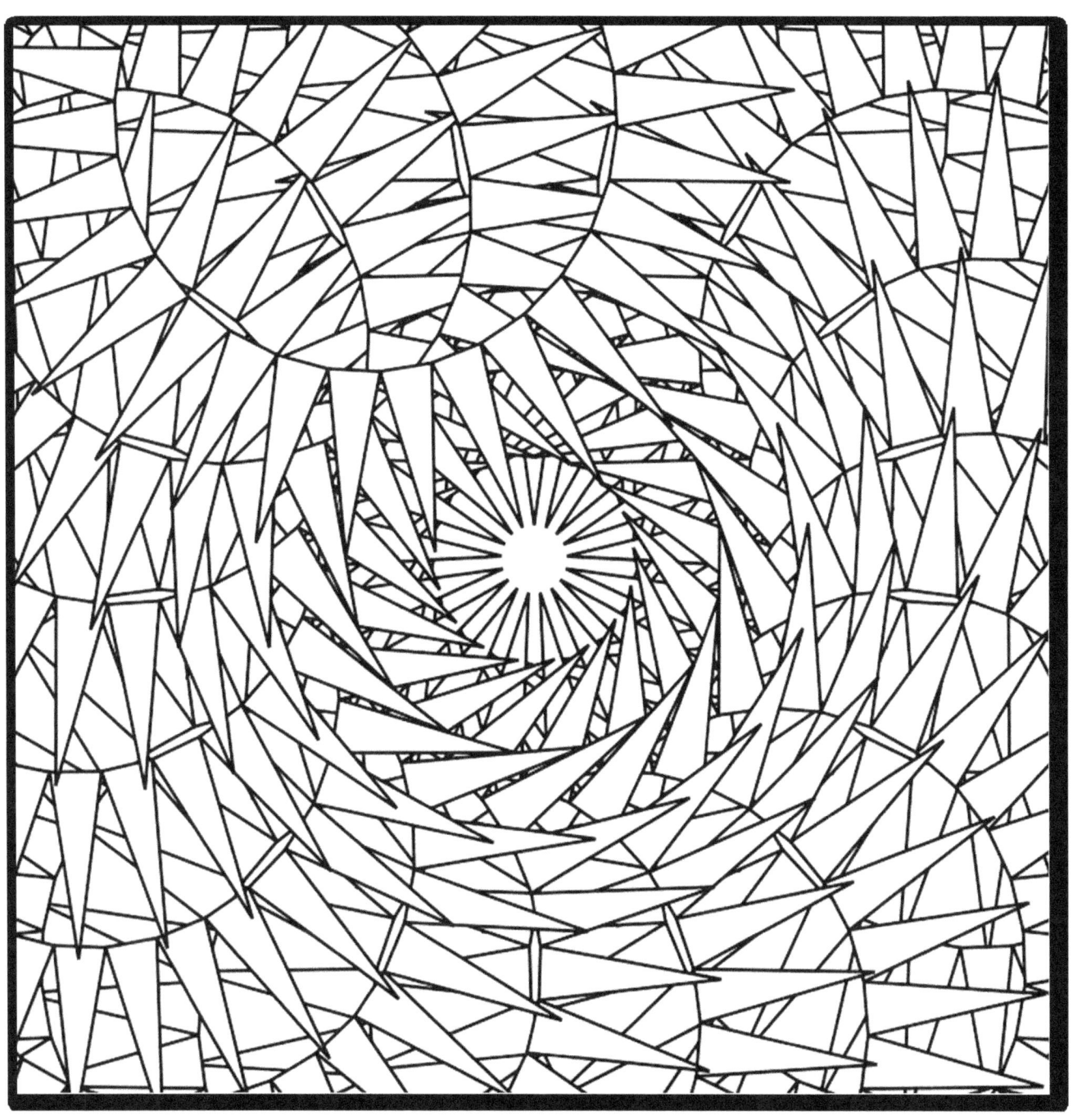

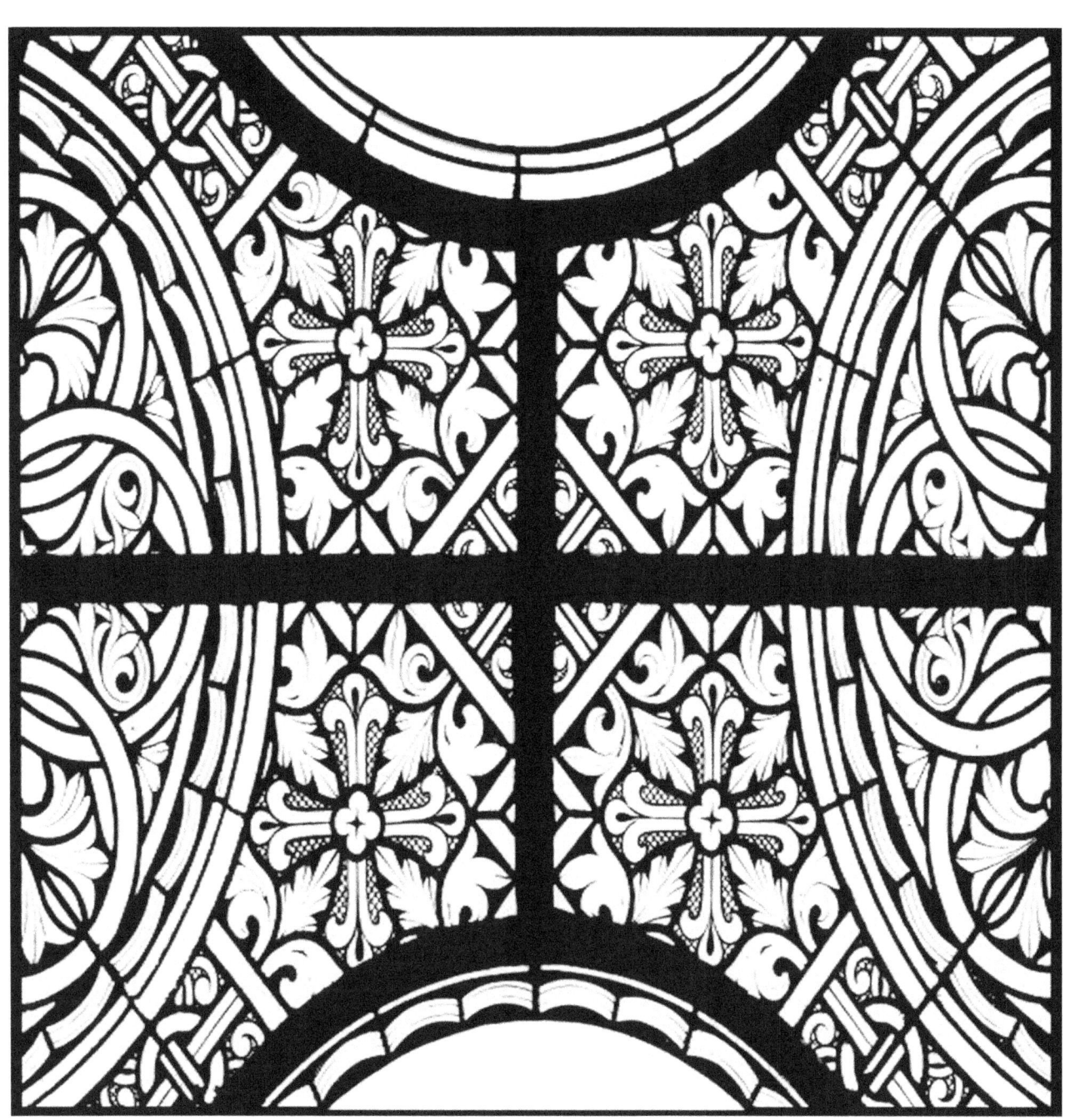

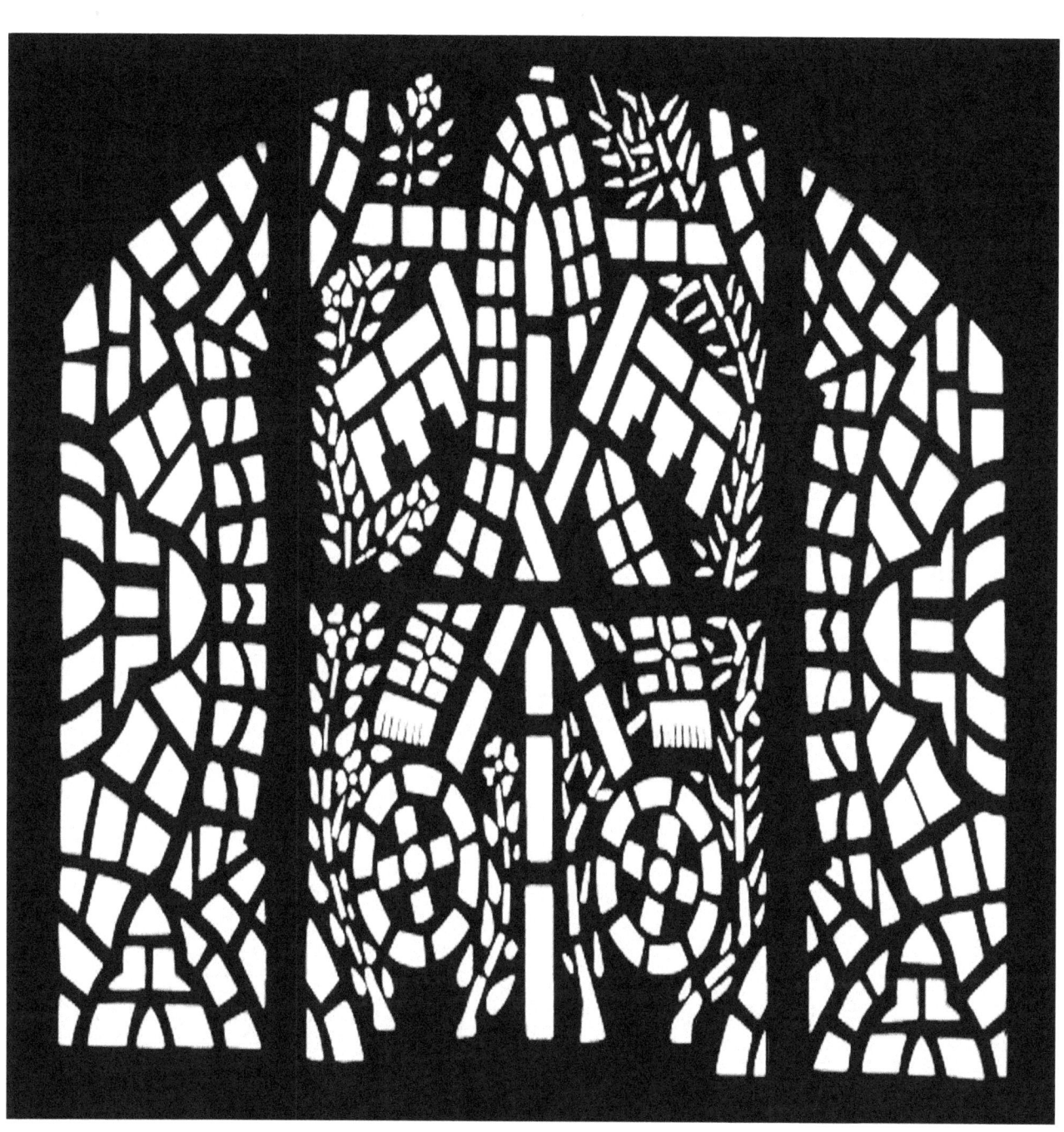

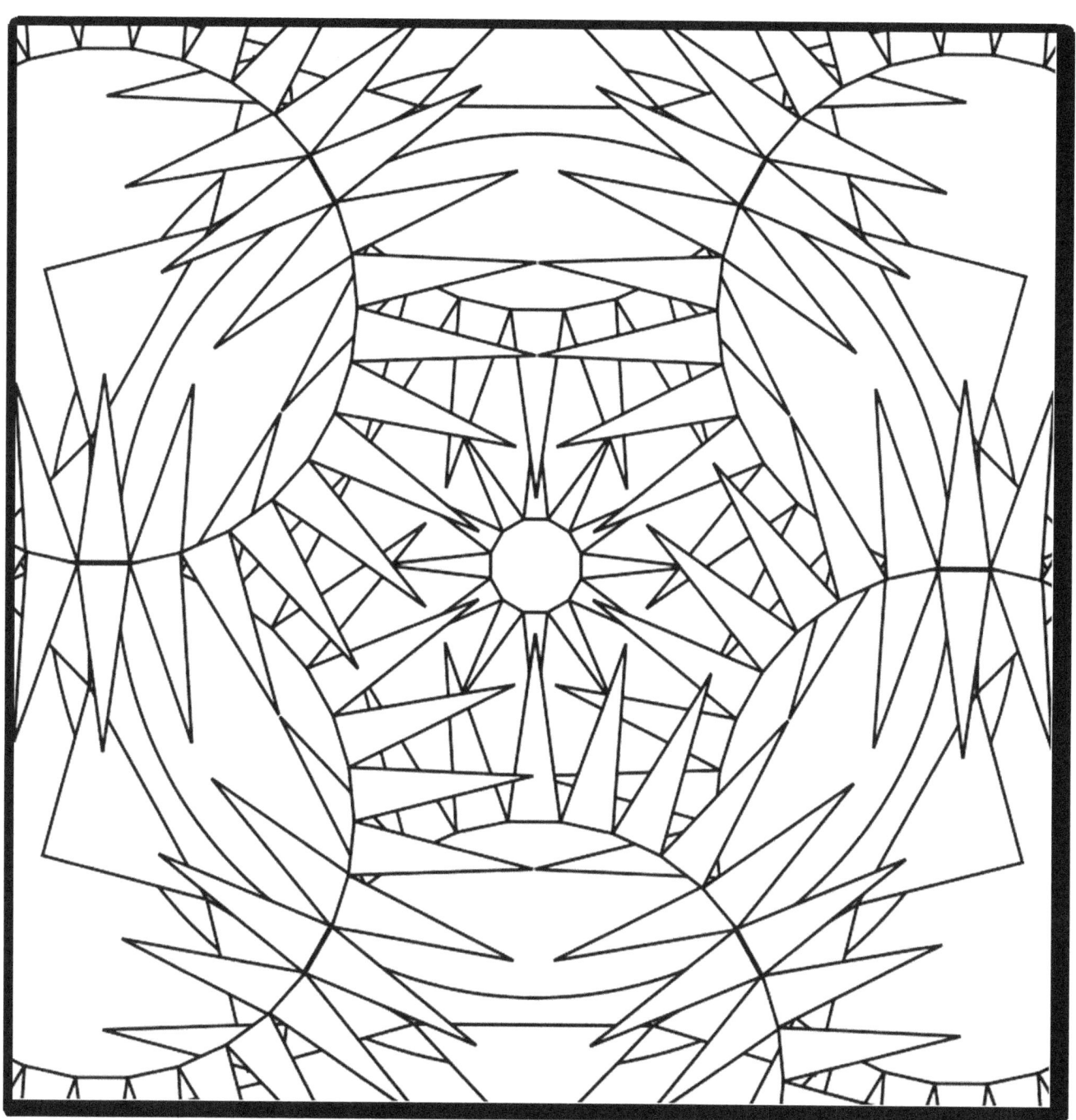

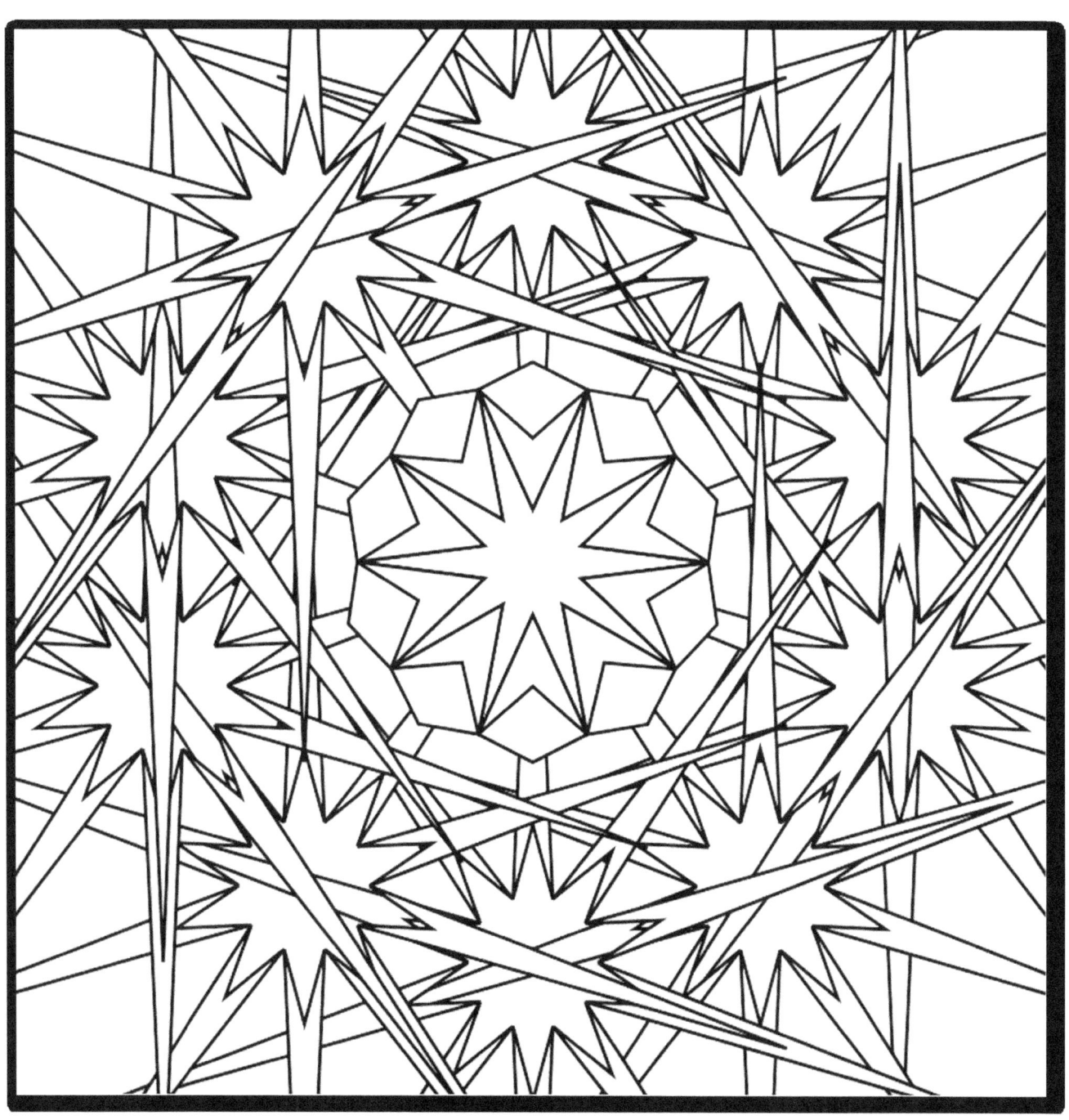

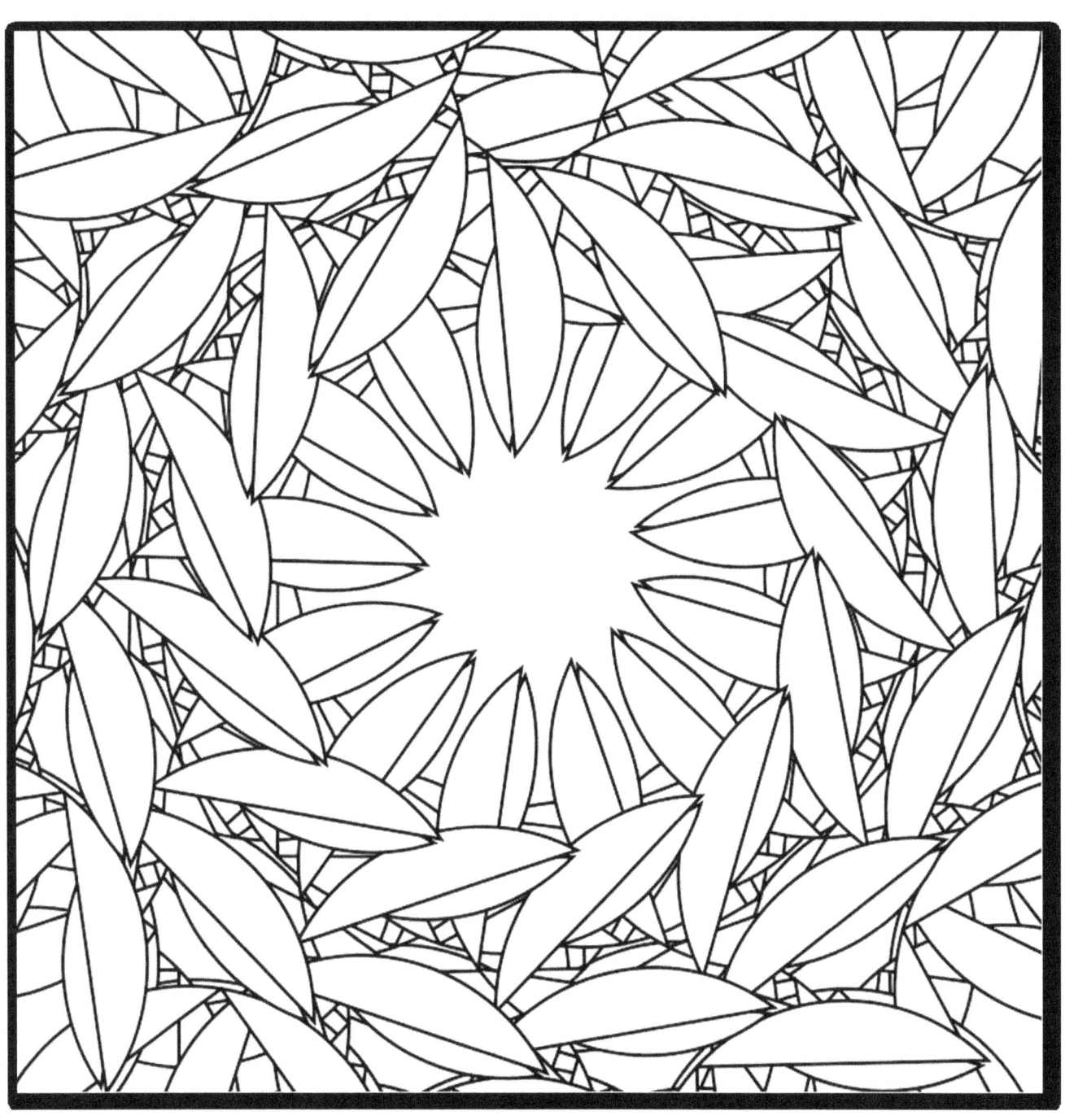

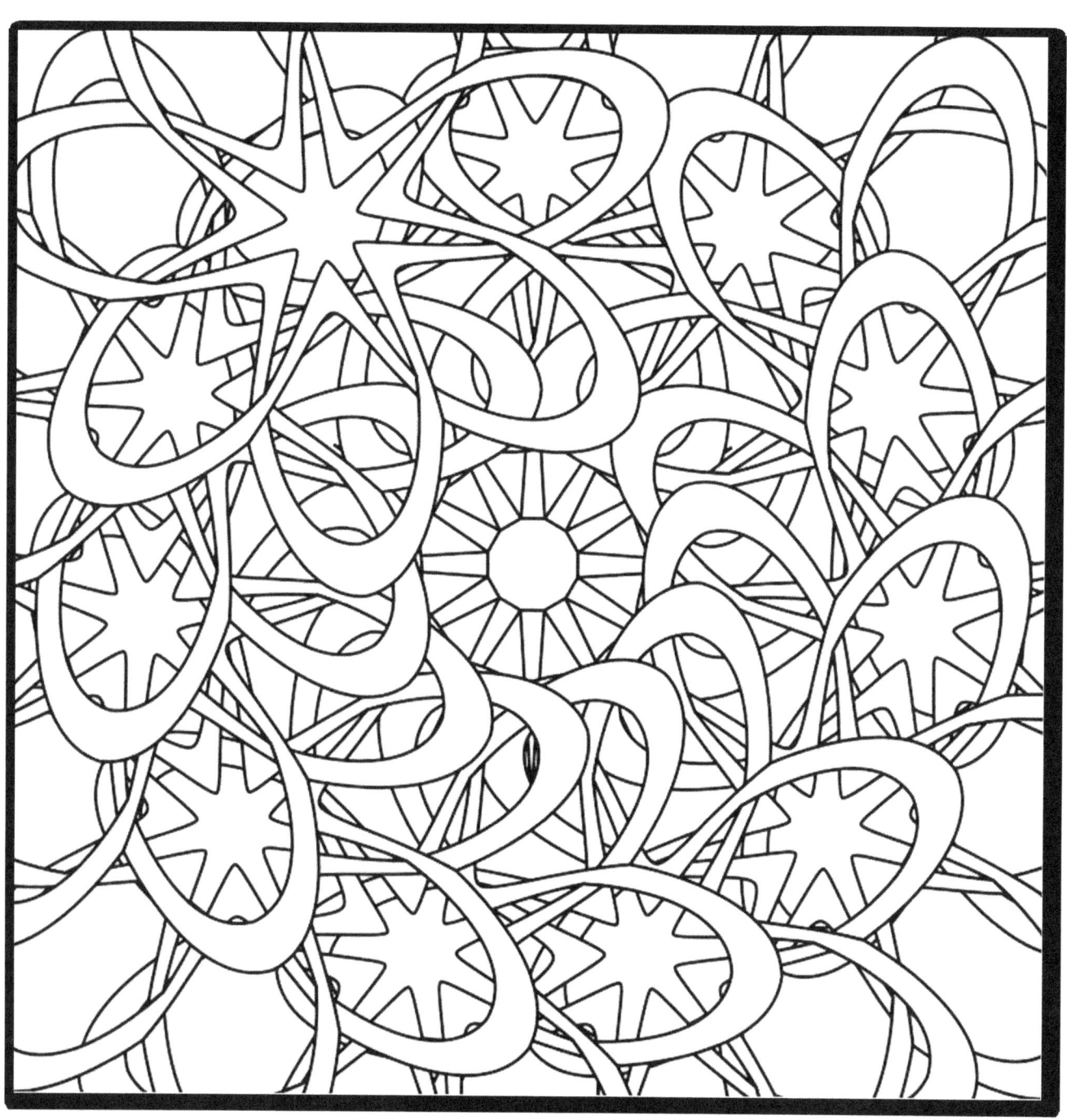

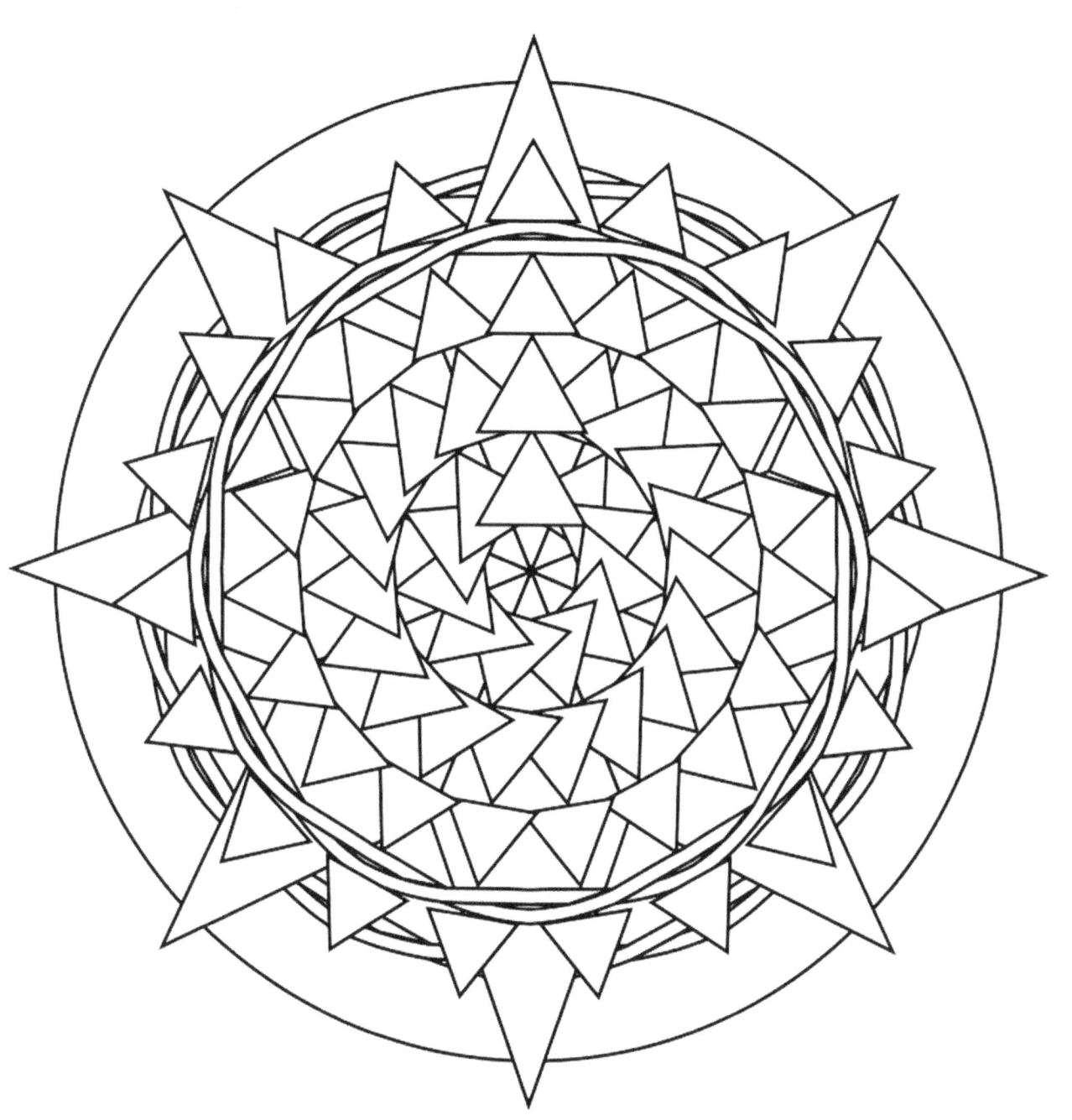

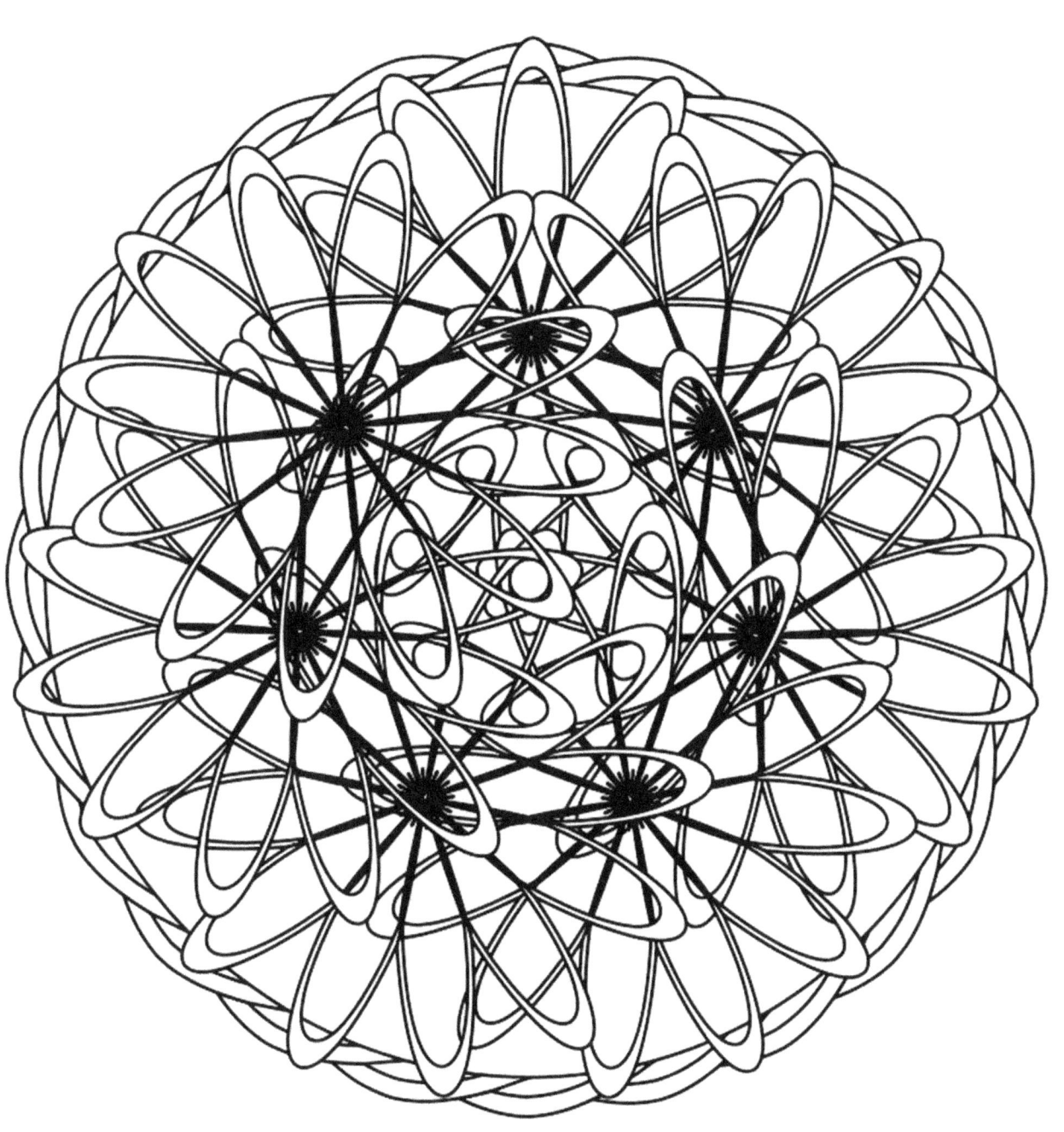

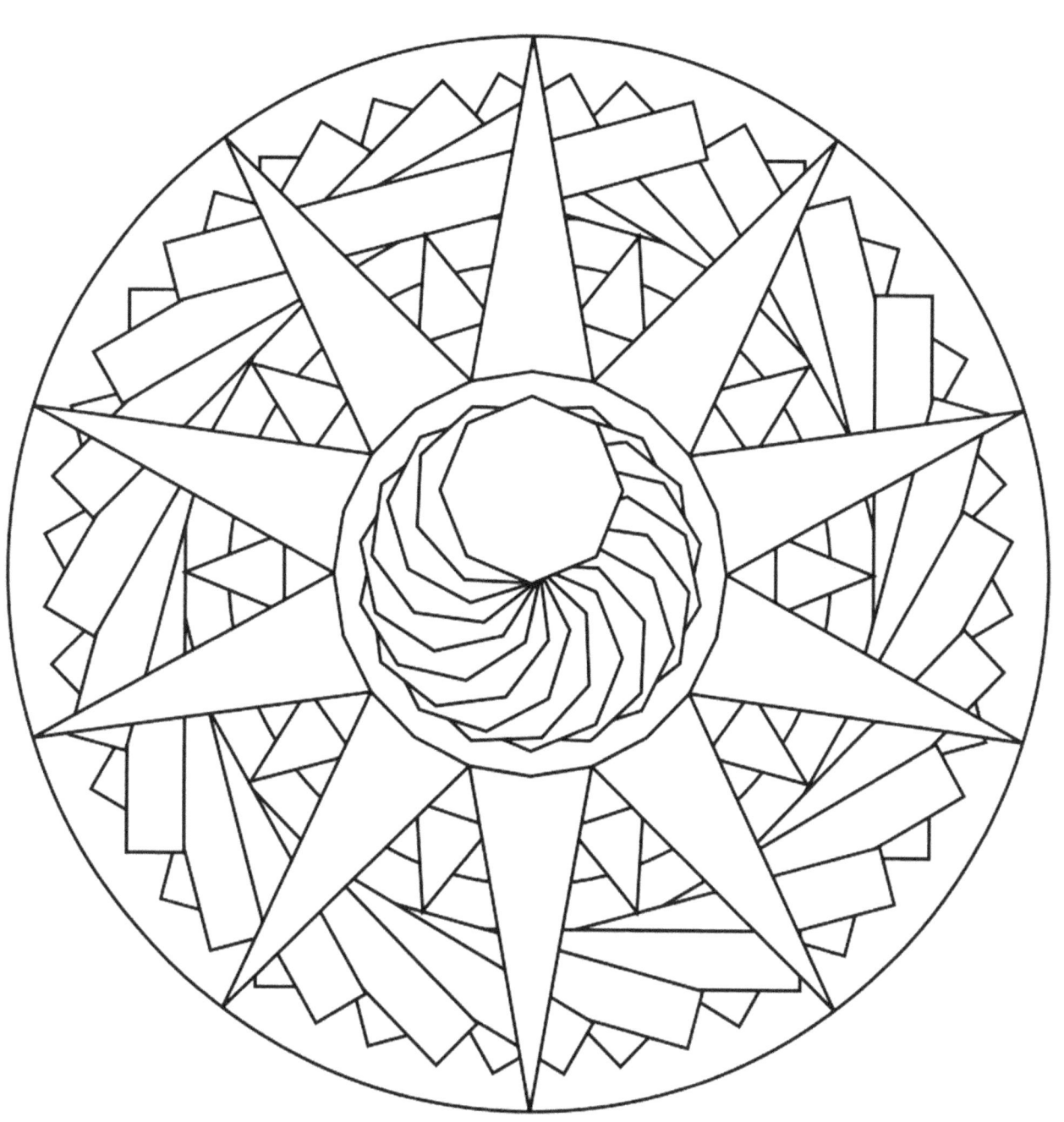

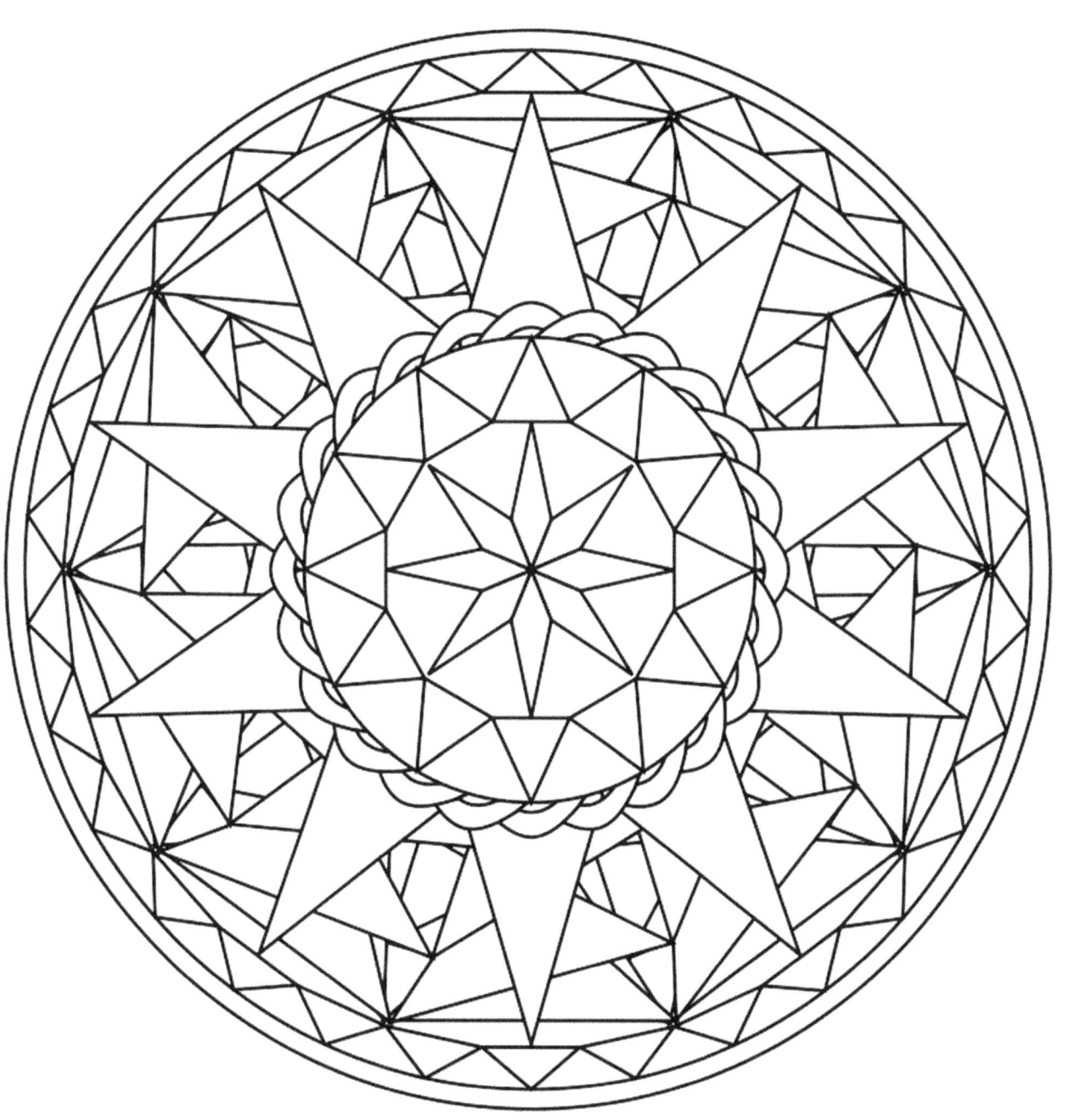

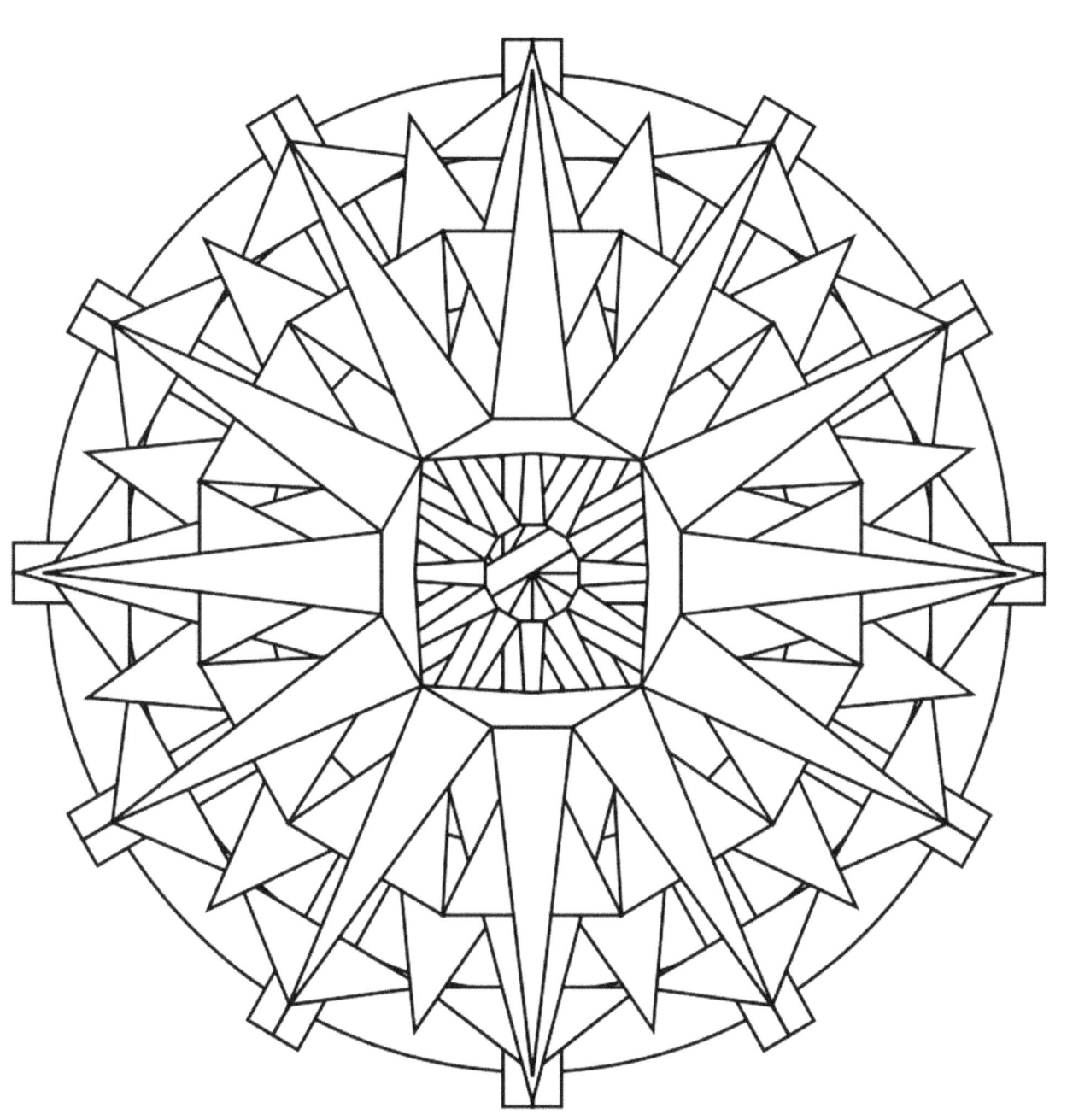

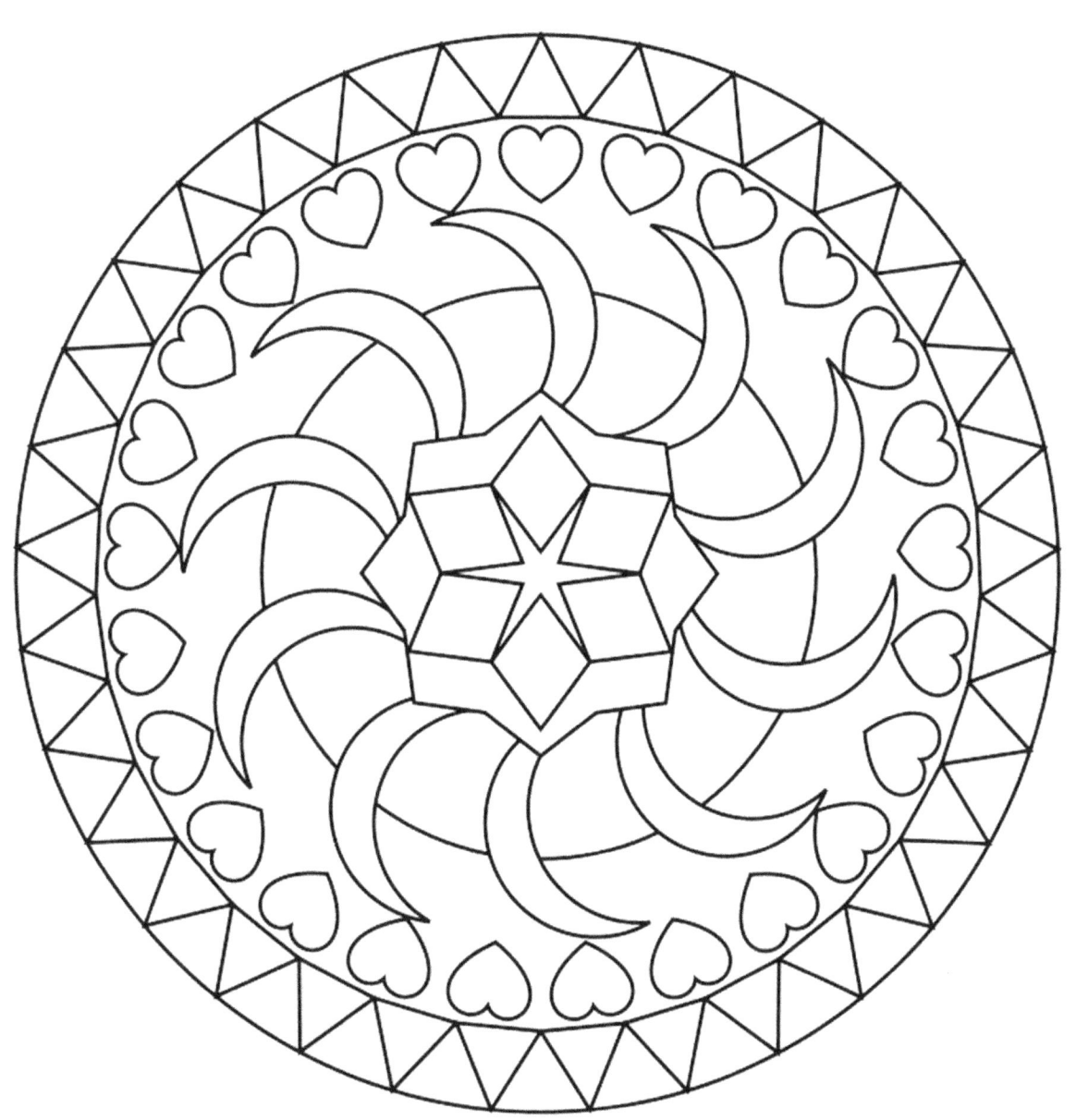

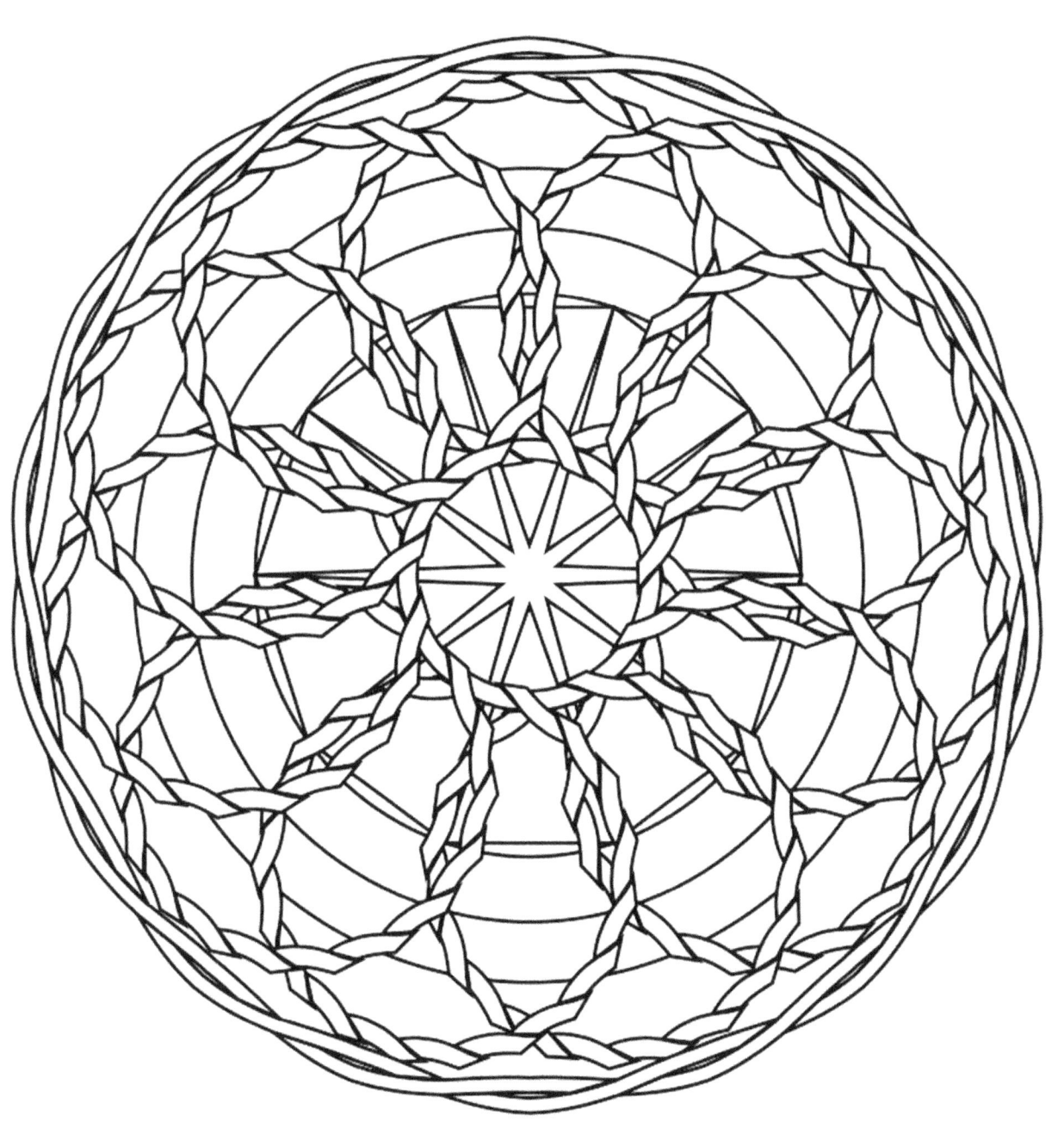

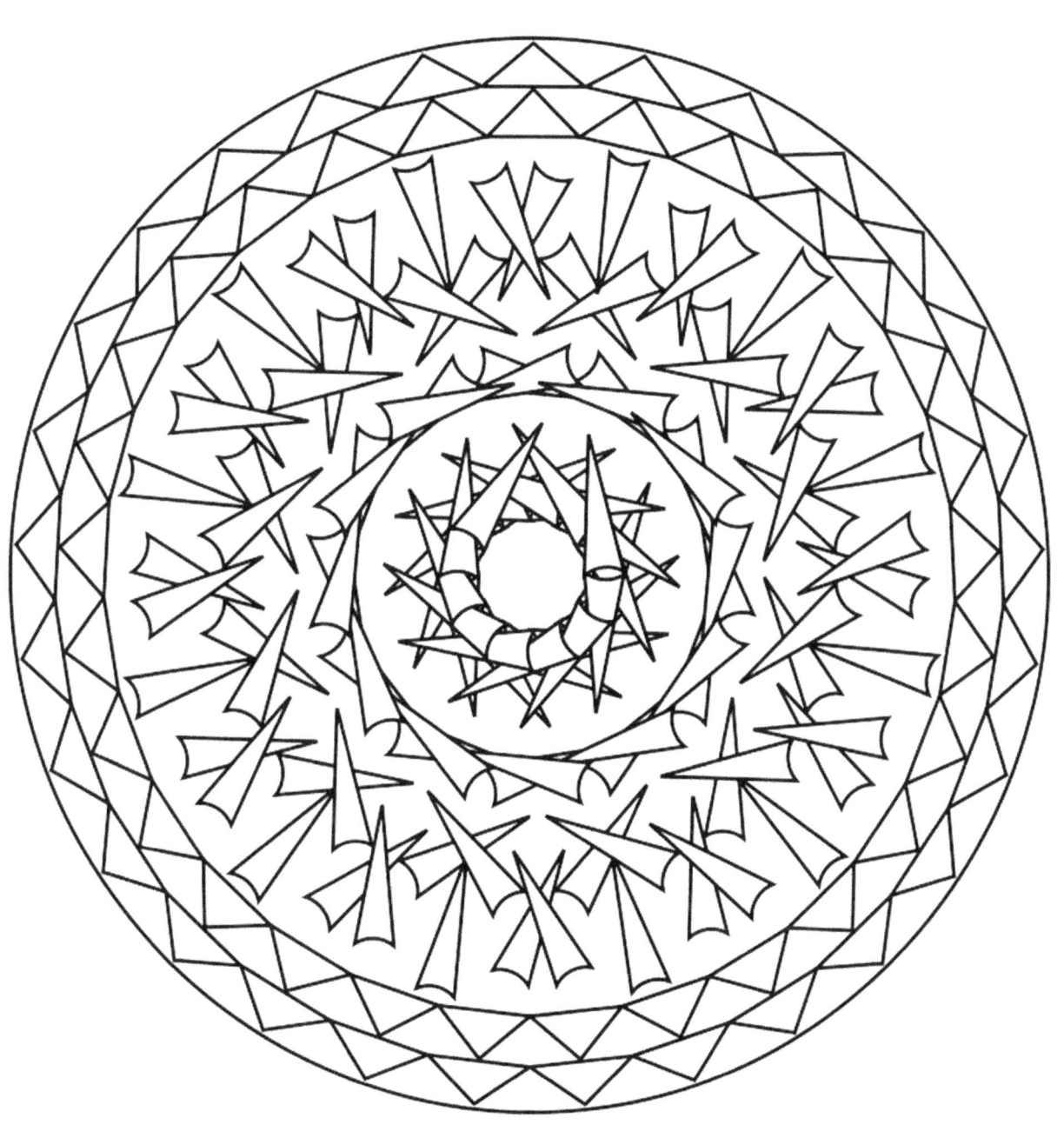

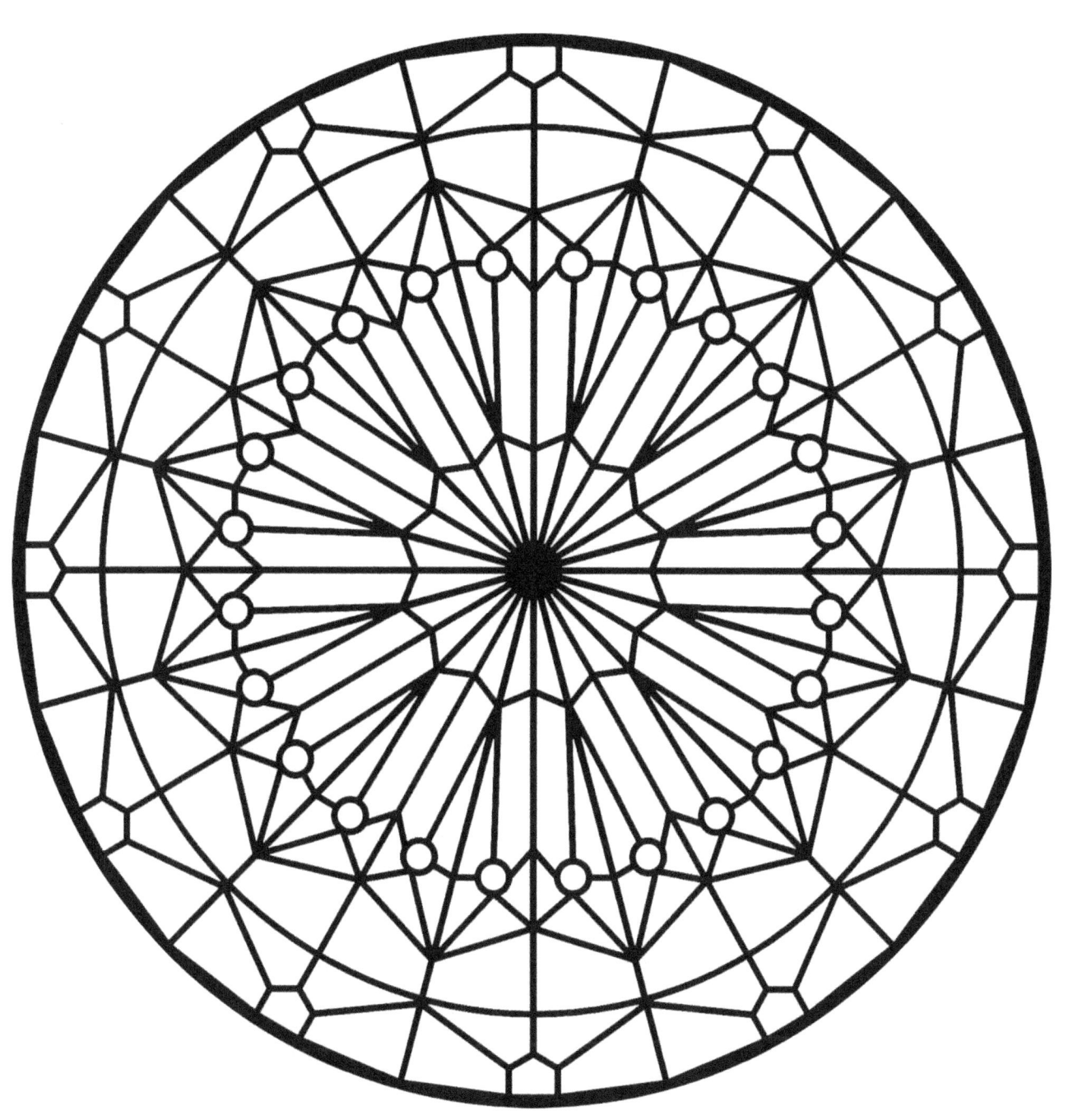

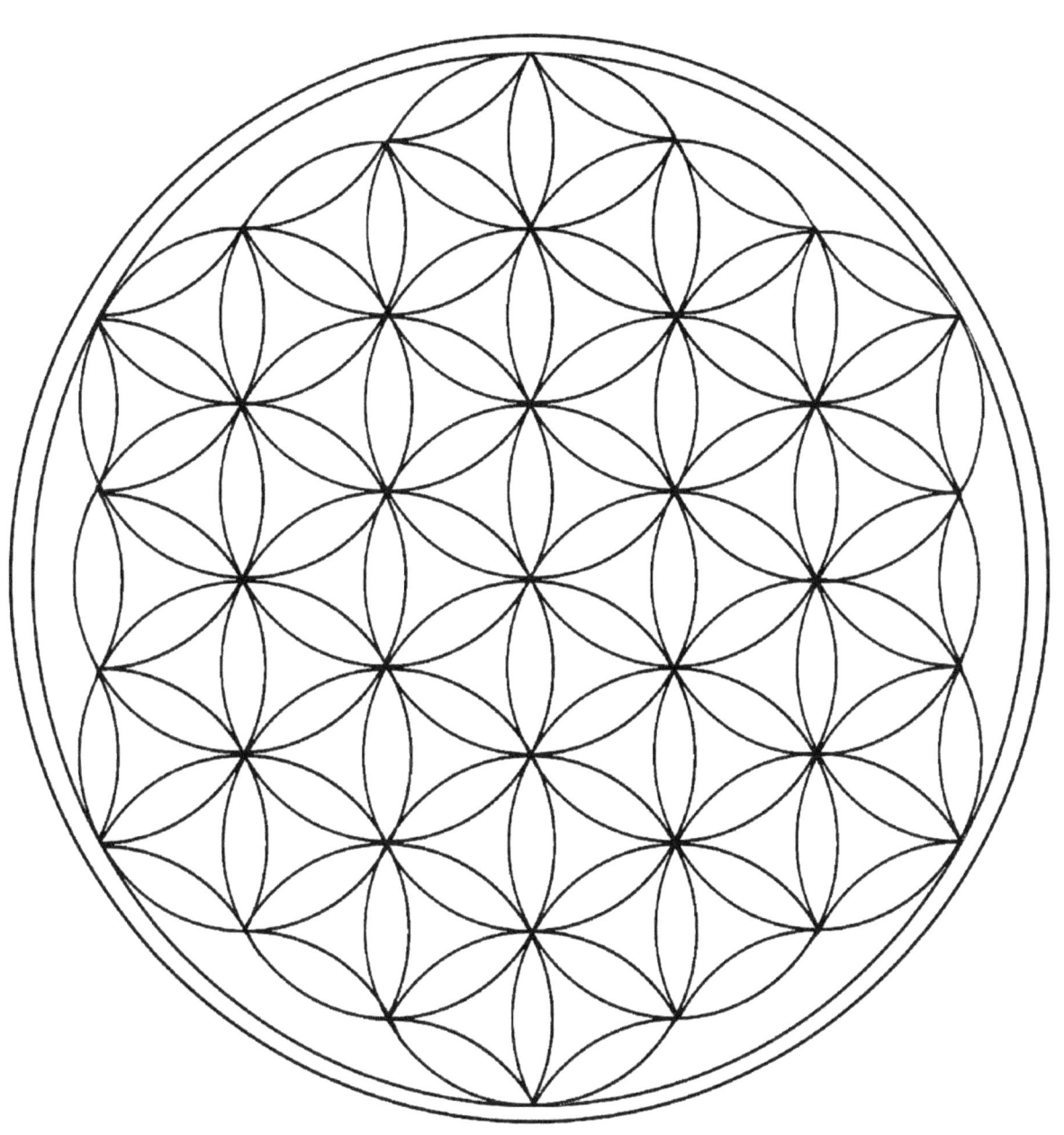

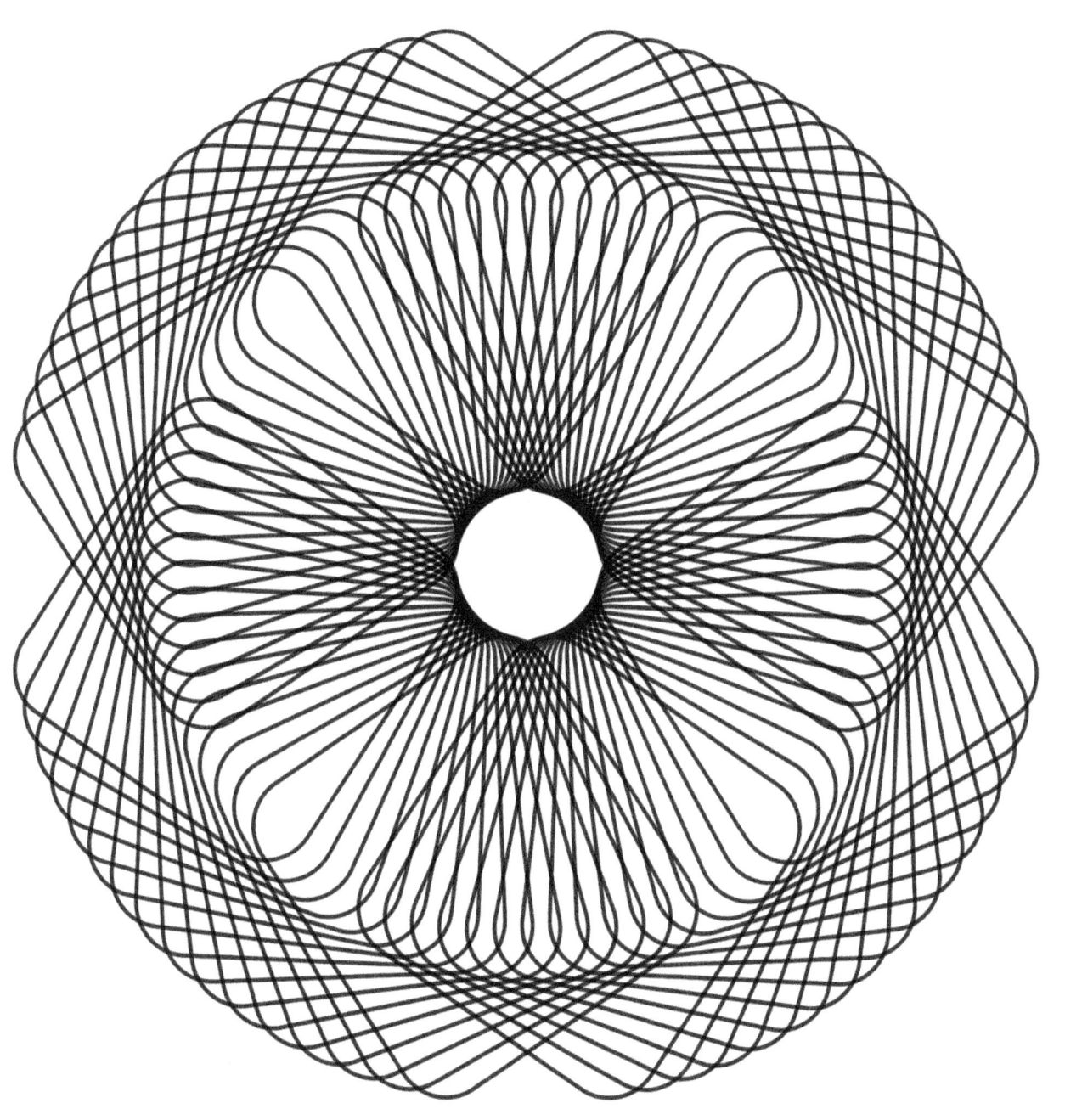

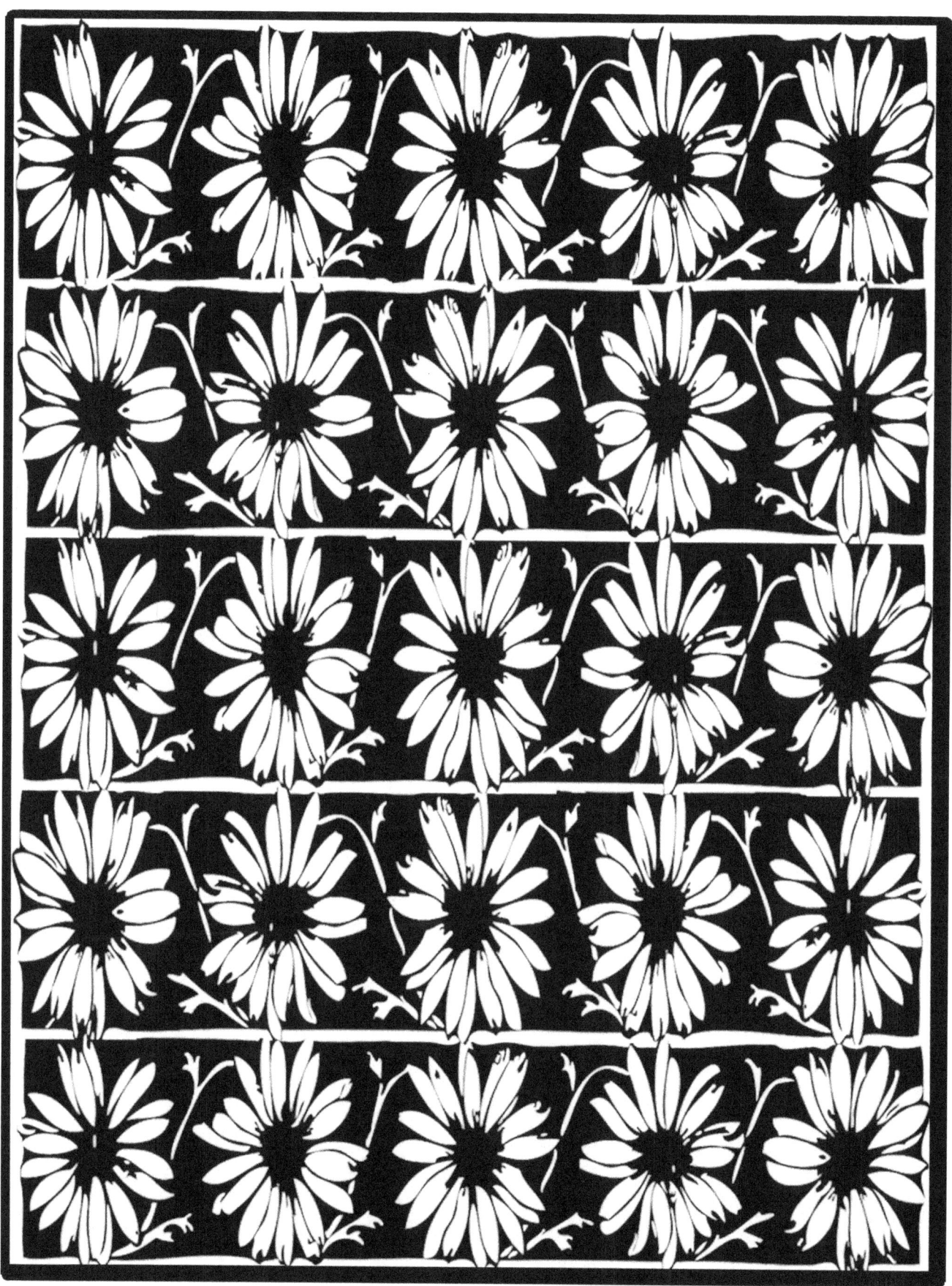

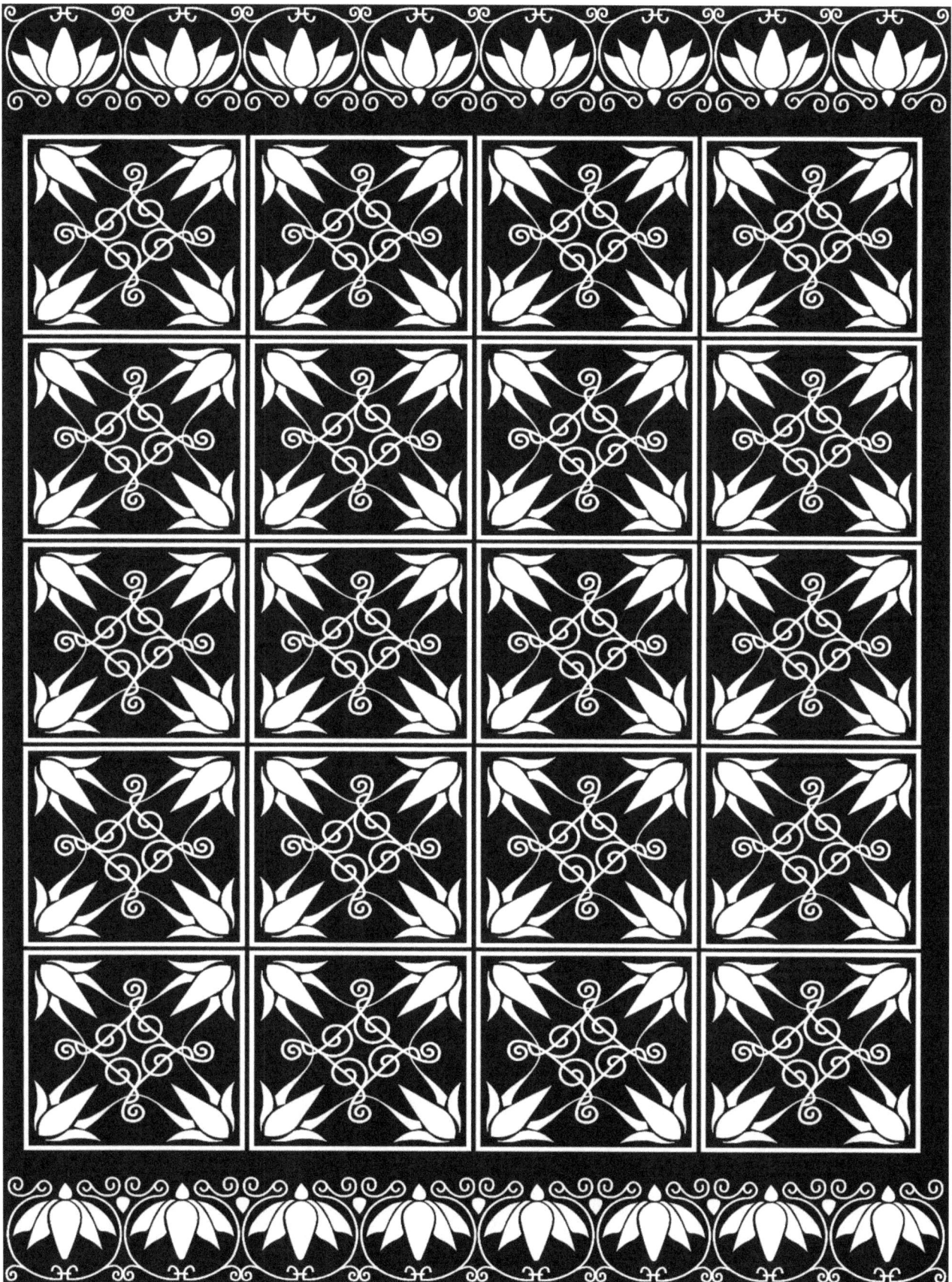

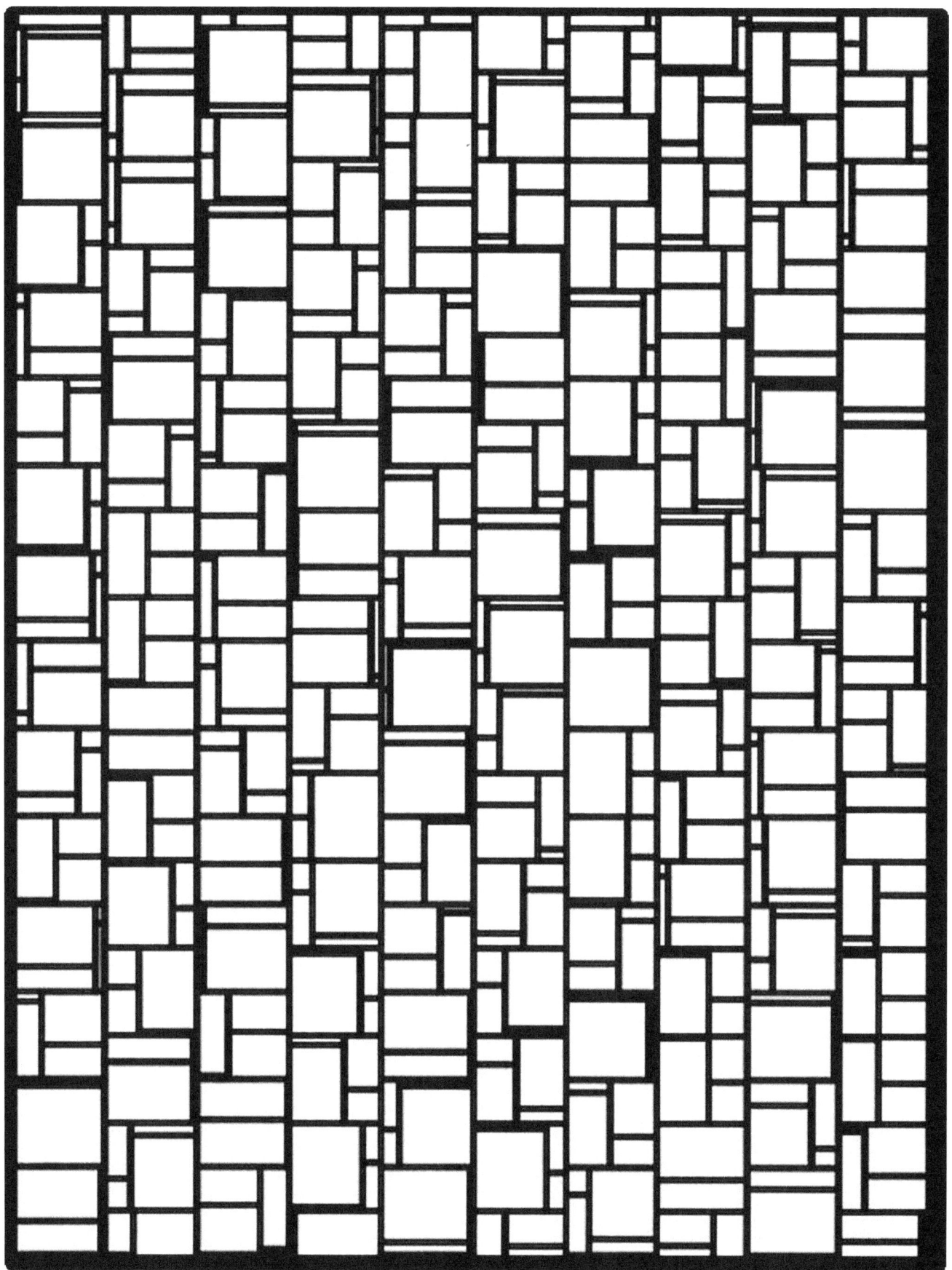

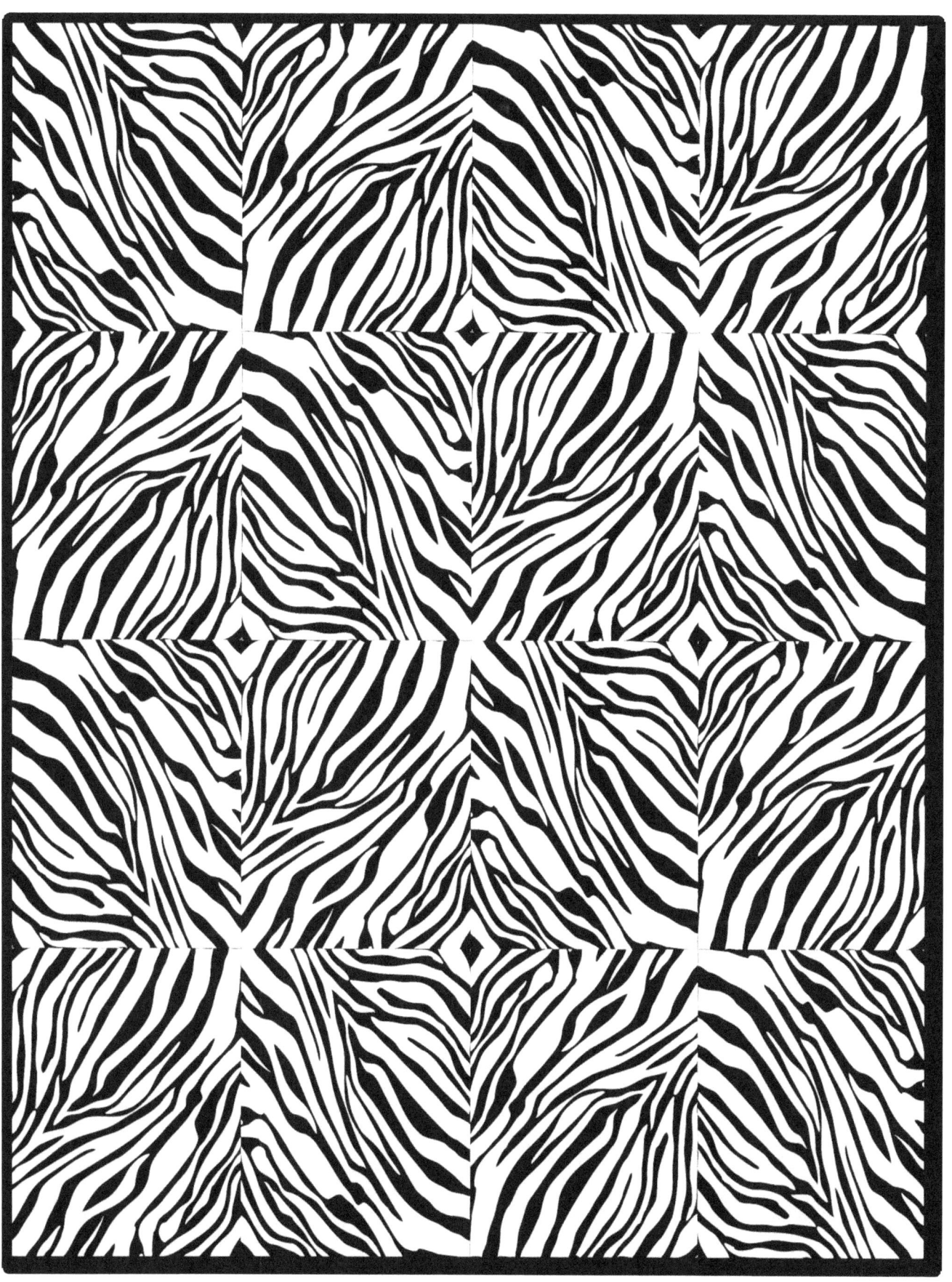

Want More Patterns?

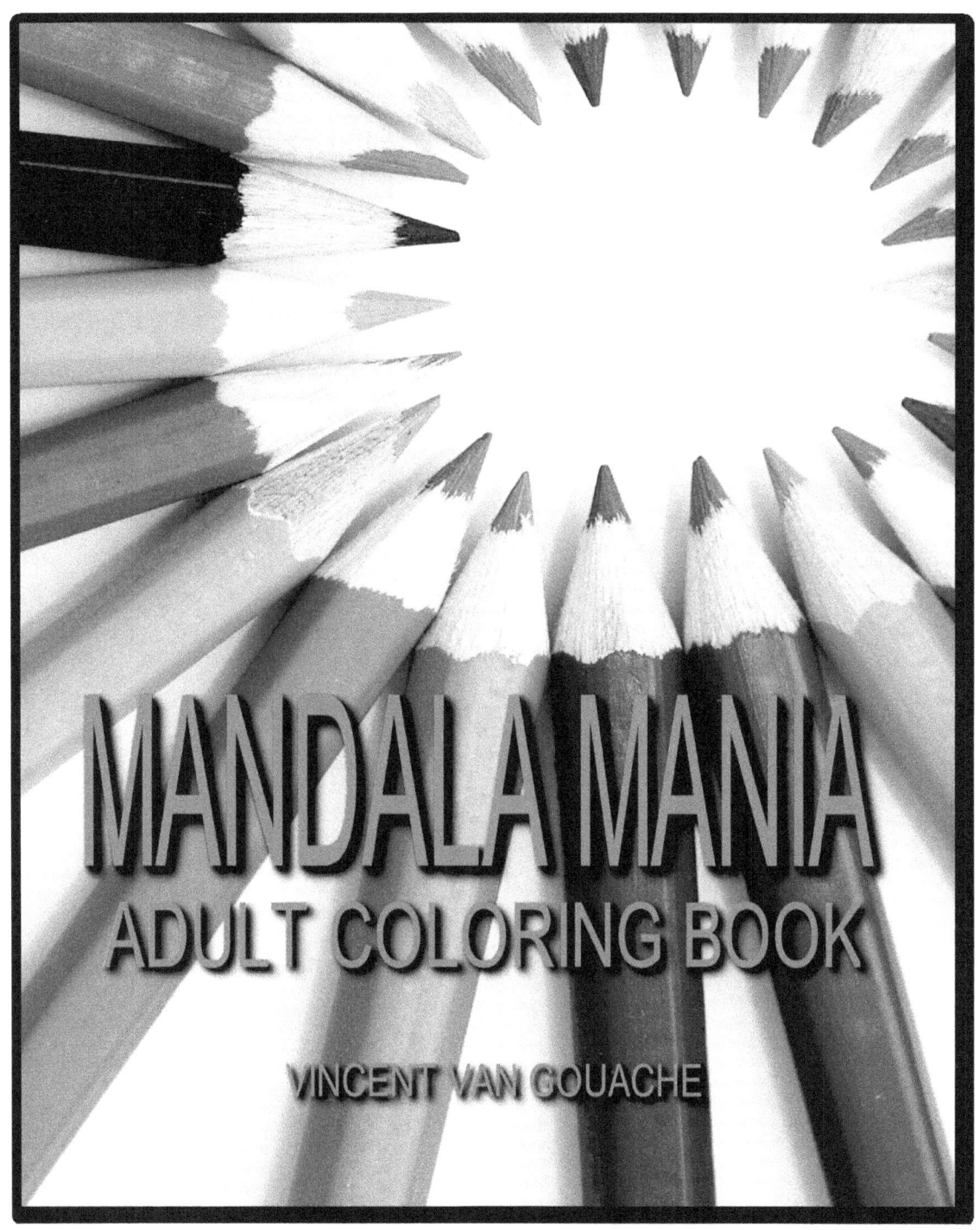

MANDALA MANIA
ADULT COLORING BOOK

VINCENT VAN GOUACHE

Available from Amazon.com
24 Original Patterns PLUS 4 bonus patterns.